PASTA
COOKBOOK

PASTA & NOODLES FROM AROUND THE WORLD WITH SAUCES TO MIX AND MATCH

Judi Olstein

Photographs by George G. Wieser

Distributed by Book Club of America
150 Motor Parkway
Hauppague, NY 11788
Tel: 516-434-1932
Fax: 516-434-4865

Produced by The Triangle Group, Ltd.
227 Park Avenue
Hoboken, NJ 07030

Design: Tony Meisel
Food styling and art direction: Brock Houghten
Special thanks to Broadway Panhandler and Margot Hughes
Origination and printing: Paramount Printing Group Ltd.

Printed in Hong Kong

ISBN 0-944297-11-0

Contents

Introduction

America is pasta crazy! Every restaurant serves pasta in guises that range from traditional Italian to Thai, Chinese, Japanese, Greek, French, North African and Latin American. Every form of dried dough we call pasta is gilded with simple to outlandish sauces, meats, vegetables, poultry and sea food.

Pasta is quick to prepare, nutritious, low in fat and capable of endless uses. It's very hard to tire of eating pasta. There's something elemental about it, like rice and potatoes, that makes it welcome at most any meal.

And pasta is so adaptable. It can be served with literally hundreds of sauces: tomato, cream, broth, vegetable, meat, seafood and fish, cheese and more.

But the best thing about pasta is that it's tasty, healthy and cheap! A meal can be thrown together in 20 minutes, including a simple sauce. Despite years of slow-simmered red sauces, most pasta sauces are actually 5-10 minute affairs, and the quicker sauces have the distinct advantage of tasting fresher and lighter.

In our house we eat pasta 2 or 3 times a week, either as an appetizer, a main course or a salad. So enter the world of pasta and enjoy!

NOTE: All the recipes call for cooking the pasta in a large pot of boiling salted water. A minimum of 4 quarts should be allowed for 1 pound of dry pasta. The pasta should be plunged into the water and the pot covered again until the water returns to the boil. Timing depends on the thickness, age and shape of the pasta, so start testing a strand or piece after 5 minutes. When the pasta is *al dente*, literally 'to the tooth' (just soft enough so it still has some resistance to the teeth) it is done. It will continue to cook after it is drained from the internal heat. When done to your taste, drain immediately, place in a serving bowl and toss with a spoonful of olive oil or butter, then pour the sauce over. Do *not* rinse pasta after draining, it will lose body and flavor.

Fresh pasta needs much less cooking, only 2–5 minutes, and less water can be used. It should never boil as the fresh pasta would disintegrate. The other rules above apply.

Left: Some of the many ingredients that can go into pasta sauces

Following pages: dry pasta, from left—fettucine, spaghetti, penne

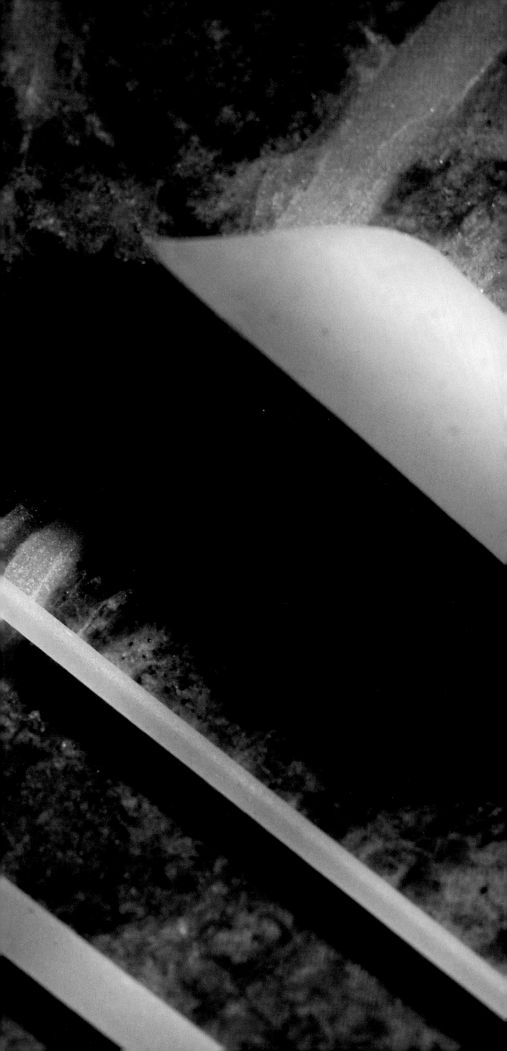

Spaghetti with Oil and Garlic

1 pound thin spaghetti
2 to 3 tablespoons olive oil
5-6 cloves or garlic, finely chopped
salt to taste
black pepper to taste

Cook the spaghetti in a large pot of salted boiling water. Drain.

In a small skillet heat the oil. Add the garlic and quickly sauté until the garlic begins to brown.

Place the spaghetti in a serving bowl. Add the garlic and oil, toss. Season with salt and pepper. Serves 4.

Right: Spaghetti with Oil and Garlic.

Preceding pages: fresh pasta, clockwise front top left—fettucine, ravioli, tortellini and angnolotti

Spaghetti Carbonara

4 tablespoons unsalted butter
1/4 pound slab bacon or 6 slices, finely chopped
1 pound thin spaghetti
4 eggs, beaten
1/3 cup grated Parmesan or Romano cheese
2 tablespoon heavy cream
Black pepper to taste

In a skillet melt the butter. Add the bacon and cook until lightly brown and keep warm.

Cook the spaghetti in a large pot of salted boiling water. Drain. Make sure the pasta stays hot. This guarantees that the eggs will be cooked.

While the pasta is cooking, combine the beaten eggs, the cheese and the cream in a serving bowl. Add to the spaghetti and toss well. Top with the cooked bacon and butter and back pepper and toss until well mixed. Serve immediately. Sprinkle with additional cheese if desired. Serves 4.

Left: Spaghetti Carbonara

Fettuccine Alfredo

1 pound fettuccine
4 tablespoons sweet butter, at room temperature
2 tablespoons heavy cream, slightly heated
1/2 cup grated Parmesan cheese
black pepper to taste

Cook the fettuccine in a pot of salted boiling water. Drain and keep warm.

While the pasta is cooking, cut the butter into bite size pieces and place in the bottom of a warm serving bowl.

After draining the pasta, add it to the bowl with the butter. Immediately add the heavy cream and cheese. Add black pepper to taste and toss well. Serves 4.

Right: Fettucine Alfredo

Elbows with Fresh Herbs and Cheese

1 pound elbow macaroni
3/4 cup sweet butter
2 cloves of garlic, crushed
2 tablespoons fresh basil, finely chopped
1 tablespoon fresh mint, finely chopped.
1/4 cup grated Parmesan cheese
1/4 cup grated Romano cheese

Cook the pasta in a pot of salted boiling water. Drain.

While the pasta is cooking, melt the butter in a skillet ; add the garlic, basil and mint. Sauté for 1-2 minutes.

Add the drained pasta to the skillet and mix well until covered with butter and herbs. Add the cheeses and mix gently but quickly. Season with fresh black pepper. Serve at once. Serves 4.

Left: Elbows with Fresh Herbs and Cheese

Lasagna

2 tablespoons olive oil
1/2 pound ground beef
1/2 pound ground pork or sweet or hot Italian sausage
  meat, out of the casing
1 large onion, chopped
2 cloves of garlic, chopped
2 large cans imported Italian tomatoes, drained
  (reserve juice)
1 cup tomato sauce
2 tablespoons tomato paste
2 tablespoons fresh basil, chopped
1 tablespoon fresh oregano, chopped
salt and pepper to taste
1 1/2 pounds lasagna
1 pound ricotta cheese
1/4 cup grated Parmesan cheese
1/4 cup grated Romano cheese
1 pound fresh mozzarella, shredded

In a large saucepan, heat the olive oil; add the ground beef, ground pork or sausage, onion, and garlic. Sauté over a medium heat until the meats are browned; about 8-10 minutes.

Add to the saucepan the tomatoes, tomato sauce, tomato paste, basil and oregano. Cook, stirring often, over a medium heat until the sauce has cooked down and is beginning to thicken. This may take 2 hours.

In a large pot of salted boiling water cook the lasagna, being careful not to break them. Drain when done and place them in a bowl of cold water until ready to use.

Combine the ricotta, Parmesan and Romano cheese together in bowl, set aside.

Preheat the oven to 350 degrees F. Lightly grease a 9 x 13-inch baking pan. To the pan add enough of the tomato sauce mixture to coat. Take the lasagna noodles from the water and drain on towels. Place the noodles, so they overlap on the bottom of the pan.

Spoon half the cheese mixture on top of the noodles. Follow with additional sauce and half of the fresh shredded mozzarella.

Repeat this process to make one more layer.

Place the pan in the oven and bake for 50-60 minutes or until hot and bubbly. Serves 6.

Spaghetti with Tomato Sauce

1 pound spaghetti
2 tablespoons olive oil
3 cloves of garlic, finely chopped
2 pounds fresh tomatoes, chopped and seeded or 1 large
  can imported Italian tomatoes, drained
1/4 cup chopped fresh basil
1/4 cup chopped fresh arugula
2 tablespoons chopped parsley
salt to taste
black pepper to taste
freshly grated Parmesan cheese, optional

In a large skillet, heat the oil. Add the garlic and sauté for 1-2 minutes. Add the tomatoes and cook uncovered over a low heat for 15-20 minutes or until the sauce begins to boil and thicken. Keep hot.

Cook the pasta in a pot of boiling salted water. Drain.

Add the basil, arugula and parsley to the sauce. Stir well. Place the pasta in a serving bowl. Toss with the sauce and season to taste with salt and pepper. Sprinkle with cheese if desired. Serves 4.

Following page: Spaghetti with Tomato Sauce

Pasta with Chicken Livers, Tomatoes and Garlic

1/2 pound fresh chicken livers
3 tablespoons olive oil
2 cloves garlic, peeled and chopped
1 large can imported Italian plum tomatoes, drained
1 teaspoon grated lemon peel
1 teaspoon fresh rosemary, chopped
2 tablespoons Marsala wine
salt and pepper to taste
1 pound bucatini or spaghetti

Clean the chicken livers and cut into small pieces.

Heat the olive oil in a saucepan and add the chopped garlic. Let brown lightly over medium heat. Add the tomatoes and mash roughly with the back of a wooden spoon. Add the lemon peel, rosemary, salt and pepper and let simmer for 15 minutes.

Cook the pasta in a pot of boiling salted water. Drain.

Just before serving add the marsala to the sauce and simmer for 2 minutes. Pour over the drained pasta and serve immediately with grated Parmesan cheese on the side. Serves 4.

Following page: Pasta with Chicken Livers, Tomatoes and Garlic

Rice Noodles with Peanut-Ginger Sauce

This refreshing dish can be served as an appetizer or as part of an oriental buffet. The fish sauce and noodles can be bought in larger supermarkets and oriental shops.

8 ounce package of oriental rice noodles
1 tablespoon sesame oil
2 cloves garlic, finely chopped
1 green pepper, cored, seeded and julienned
1 red pepper, cored, seeded and julienned
2 scallions, coarsely chopped
1 tablespoon fresh ginger, julienned
4-6 ounces small, cooked shrimp
2 tablespoons nam phua (Thai fish sauce)
1 tablespoon soy sauce
1/4 cup smooth peanut butter

Place noodles in a large bowl and cover with boiling water for 5 minutes.

In a saucepan, heat the sesame oil. Sauté the garlic, peppers, scallions, ginger and shrimp for 5-7 minutes over high heat, tossing constantly.

Add the fish sauce, soy sauce and peanut butter and toss well.

Drain the noodles well and place in a bowl. Pour the shrimp and vegetable mixture over and serve. Serves 4.

Following pages: Rice Noodles with Peanut-Ginger Sauce

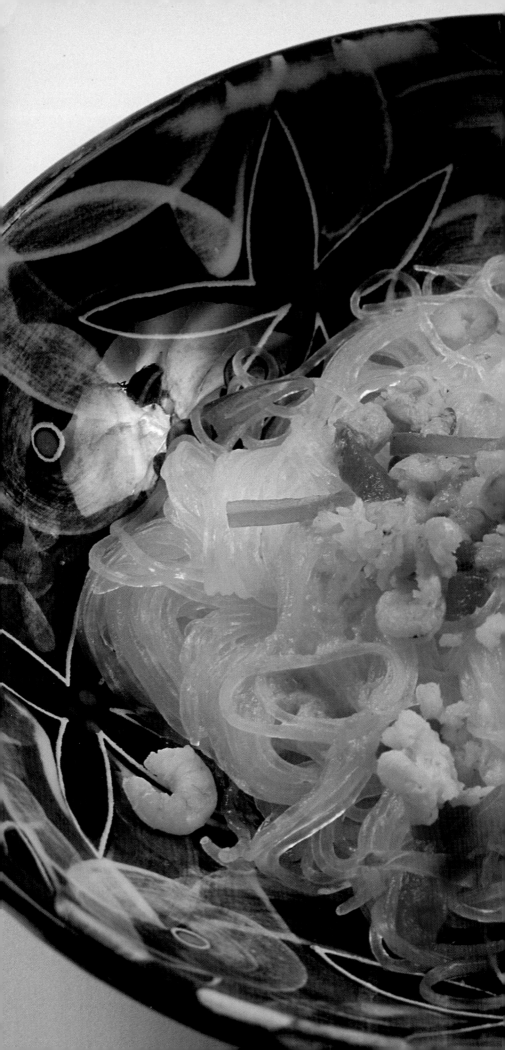

Macaroni and Cheese

The old stand-by with a new twist!

1 pound macaroni
3 tablespoons butter
3 tablespoons flour
2 cups warm milk
1 cup grated cheddar cheese
1 teaspoon Tabasco
1/2 teaspoon ground nutmeg
1 teaspoon black pepper
2 teaspoons salt

Boil the macaroni in at least 4 quarts of salted water until just firm. Drain and set aside.

In a saucepan over low heat, melt the butter. Stir in the flour and blend thoroughly. Let cook 2 minutes. Slowly add the warm milk, stirring constantly, until well blended. Add the cheese and Tabasco and continue stirring until the cheese is melted and the whole is smooth and thick.

Place the macaroni in a deep, oven-proof casserole. Pour the cheese mixture over and fold in. Place in a 400 degree F. oven for 20 minutes until hot through and browned on top. Serves 4.

Pasta with Tuna Sauce

An unusual combination, typical of the Ligurian coast of Northern Italy. It makes a fast, delicious meal, accompanied by a salad and dry white wine.

2 cloves garlic, chopped
1 7-ounce can tuna in olive oil
1 28-ounce can Italian plum tomatoes
1/2 cup fresh basil leaves, finely chopped
1 teaspoon capers, roughly chopped
1 pound penne
1/2 cup hot peas (for garnish)

First, make the sauce. Sauté garlic in the oil drained from the tuna. Add the tomatoes and cook for two minutes over medium heat. Add the remaining ingredients, except the pasta and continue cooking for 10 minutes until well-blended and slightly reduced.

Cook the penne in plenty of boiling, salted water until *al dente*, slightly resistant to the tooth. Drain pasta and immediately place in a heated, large bowl, add the sauce and toss thoroughly. Garnish with peas. Serve immediately. Serves 4.

Following pages: Pasta with Tuna Sauce

Linguine with Clam Sauce

1/4 cup olive oil
1 medium onion, finely chopped
2 cloves of garlic, crushed
1 large can imported Italian tomatoes, drained, sieved
and mixed with juices
1/2 teaspoon oregano
2 dashes of Tabasco sauce
2 dozen cherrystone clams, shucked and coarsely chopped,
set aside in their juices
1 pound linguine

In a large skillet, heat the olive oil. Add the onions and sauté for 5 minutes or until the onions begin to wilt and become transparent. Add the garlic and cook 1 minute longer.

To the onion mixture add the tomatoes, oregano, and Tabasco; bring the mixture to a boil. Lower the heat to a simmer and continue cooking for 8-10 minutes or until the mixture begins to thicken and reduce.

Add the clams with their juices to the skillet cook over a low heat for 3-5 minutes.

Cook the linguine in a large pot of boiling salted water. Drain.

Transfer the linguine to a serving bowl and toss with some of the sauce. Spoon the rest of the sauce over the pasta and serve. Serves 4.

Right: Linguine with Clam Sauce

Spaghetti with Broccoli, Garlic and Oil

1 pound or 1 large bunch of broccoli
1/4 cup olive oil
4 cloves of garlic, finely chopped
1 pound of penne
freshly grated Parmesan cheese, to taste
black pepper, to taste

Cook the spaghetti in a large pot of salted boiling water. Drain.

While the spaghetti is cooking, trim the broccoli and break the bunch into florets. Steam 8-10 minutes or until just tender.

While the broccoli is cooking, heat the oil in large skillet. Add the garlic and sauté briefly. When the broccoli is done, add it to the garlic oil mixture, sauté for 1-2 minutes.

Place the garlic and broccoli mixture in a large serving bowl. Add the spaghetti and toss. Sprinkle with cheese and pepper to taste. Serves 4.

Left: Spaghetti with Broccoli, Garlic and Oil

Following pages: Spaghetti with Black Olives,
Tomatoes and Anchovies

Spaghetti with Black Olives, Tomatoes and Anchovies

1/4 cup olive oil
2 cloves of garlic, finely chopped
1 can of anchovy fillets, finely chopped
1 large can of imported Italian tomatoes, drained and
*   coarsely chopped, reserve juice*
10-12 imported black olives, pitted and coarsely chopped
1/4 cup fresh basil, coarsely chopped.
1 pound of spaghetti
black pepper to taste

In a large skillet heat the olive oil and stir in the garlic and anchovies. Cook until anchovies begin to disintegrate; about 2 minutes. Add the tomatoes and some of their juice, the olives and basil. Simmer the mixture over a medium heat, stirring occasionally, until the sauce thickens only slightly.

While the sauce is simmering, cook the spaghetti in a large pot of salted boiling water. Drain.

Transfer the spaghetti to a serving bowl and toss with the sauce. Season with pepper to taste. Serves 4.

Pasta with Four Cheeses

1/4 cup sweet butter
2 cloves of garlic, finely chopped
1 large container of ricotta cheese
1/4 cup freshly grated Romano cheese
2 tablespoons freshly grated Parmesan cheese
2 tablespoons crumbled Gorgonzola
1 pound penne, ziti or rigatoni
black pepper to taste

In a large skillet melt the butter, stir in the garlic and
sauté briefly. Add ricotta, Romano, parmesan and
Gorgonzola cheeses. Mix well. Cook the mixture over a
low heat until it is heated through, stir constantly. Keep
warm over a very low heat.

While the sauce is cooking, cook the pasta in a large
pot of boiling salted water. Drain.

Transfer the pasta to a large serving bowl and top
with the cheese sauce, coat thoroughly. Season with
black pepper. Serve immediately. Serves 4.

Following pages: Pasta with Four Cheeses

Linguine with Seafood and Basil Cream

2 tablespoons butter
2 cloves garlic, peeled and chopped
1/2 pound shrimp, cleaned and deveined
1/2 pound scallops,
  cut in halves or quarters if large
1 cup fresh basil leaves, packed
1 teaspoon green peppercorns, crushed
1 cup light cream, heated
1 pound linguine
salt and pepper to taste

Cook the pasta in a large pot of boiling, salted water until *al dente*. Drain and serve with the sauce.

In a skillet, melt the butter. Sauté garlic until lightly browned. Add the shrimp and scallops and cook over medium heat 5 minutes, until shrimp are pink and scallops opaque white. Add the basil, green peppercorns and hot cream and let simmer 5 minutes. Pour over pasta and serve immediately. Serves 4.

Right: Linguine with Seafood and Basil Cream

Twists with Chicken
and Red Peppers

2 tablespoons olive oil
1 small onion, finely chopped
2 cloves garlic, peeled and chopped
1 whole chicken breast, skinned and
*   cut into julienne strips*
2 sweet red peppers, seeded, skinned
*   and finely chopped*
1/2 cup light cream
1/2 teaspoon Tabasco sauce
1 pound twists or any other short pasta

In a large skillet, sauté the onion and garlic in the olive oil. Add the chicken and cook over medium heat, stirring often, for 5 minutes until the chicken is lightly browned.

Add the red peppers and cook for another 5 minutes until soft and blended. Add the cream and Tabasco and simmer for 5 minutes more.

In the meantime, cook the pasta in boiling, salted water. Drain. Pour over the sauce, toss well and serve. Grated Romano cheese is a good addition. Serves 4.

Left: Twists with Chicken and Red Peppers

Cannelloni

Cannelloni can be made from either of two types of pasta: dried, cooked, split and stuffed or with fresh pasta dough cut into rounds or squares, lightly cooked and then rolled-up like crepes or pancakes. Either works well for this recipe.

1 onion, chopped
1 clove garlic, peeled and chopped
1/2 pound ground veal
2 anchovy filets, chopped
1 teaspoon capers, chopped
6 oil-cured black olives, pitted and chopped
1 tablespoon chopped fresh basil
1 tablespoon extra virgin olive oil
1 egg
8 cannelloni
2 cups light tomato sauce
1/2 cup Parmesan cheese, grated

In a large mixing bowl combine the onion, garlic, veal, anchovy, capers, olives, basil, olive oil and egg. Mix lightly yet thoroughly. Use this mixture to stuff the cannelloni.

Place the pasta tubes in a greased baking dish, cover with the tomato sauce and dust heavily with grated Parmesan cheese. Bake in a 400 degree F. oven for 20-25 minutes until the pasta is piping hot and the cheese is lightly browned. Serves 4.

Right: Cannelloni

Shells with Vodka Cream

1 pound pasta shells, large or small
1 tablespoon butter
1 clove garlic, peeled and chopped
1 tomato, peeled, seeded and chopped
1/4 pound shrimp, crushed into a paste
1/4 cup vodka
1 cup heavy cream
salt and pepper to taste

Cook the pasta shells in boiling, salted water until done. Drain.

Meanwhile, sauté the garlic in the butter in a skillet. Add the tomato and shrimp paste and cook for 5 minutes over medium heat, stirring constantly. Add the vodka and let cook for 2 minutes to evaporate the alcohol and blend the tastes. Finally, add the cream and simmer for 5 minutes. Pour over the pasta and serve. Serves 4.

Right: Shells with Vodka Cream

Shells with Ricotta
and Fresh Vegetables

1 pound spinach linguine
1 pound ricotta cheese
1 teaspoon fresh oregano or marjoram, finely chopped
2 tablespoons butter
2 tablespoons olive oil
2 tomatoes, peeled, seeded and roughly chopped
1 small zucchini, in julienne
1 carrot, in julienne
1 onion, thinly sliced
1 cup thinly sliced mushrooms
1 cup broccoli flowerets
1/2 cup grated Parmesan cheese
salt and pepper to taste

Cook the shells in boiling, salted water until just slightly underdone. Drain and let cool slightly.

Mix the ricotta and oregano together with a fork. Stuff the shells with the cheese mixture and place in a greased baking pan. Keep warm in a low oven.

In a large skillet melt the butter and oil over medium heat. Add the tomatoes, zucchini, carrot, onion and mushrooms and sauté for five minutes. Add the broccoli, cover the pan, and steam for 5 minutes. Season with salt and pepper.

Spread the vegetable mixture over the stuffed shells, sprinkle the Parmesan cheese over the top and bake for 20 minutes at 350 degrees F. Serves 4-6.

Spaghetti Primavera

There are a thousand-and-one recipes for pasta primavera (springtime). The variety of vegetables depends entirely on what's available, but all should be young and in prime condition.

2 tablespoons butter or olive oil
2 cloves garlic, peeled and chopped
1 small onion, thinly sliced
1 cup mushrooms, thinly sliced
1 small zucchini, in julienne
1 small carrot, in julienne
1 cup broccoli flowerets
2 tomatoes, peeled, seeded and chopped
1 cup string beans, sliced lengthwise
1 cup asparagus tips
1 cup light cream
1 1/2 pounds spinach spaghetti
salt and pepper to taste

Cook the spaghetti in a large pot of boiling, salted water until *al dente*. Drain and set aside. In a very large skillet or wok, heat the butter or olive oil (butter if to be eaten hot, olive oil to make into a salad).

Sauté the garlic, onions and mushrooms until soft and golden. Add all the other vegetables and toss over high heat until just crisp and hot. Add the cream and heat through. Pour over the pasta and season with salt and pepper. Serve immediately.

If you wish to make a salad to be served at room temperature, toss spaghetti with vegetables, leave out the cream and add another 1/2 cup of olive oil and vinegar to taste and let marinate for an hour before serving. Serves 6.

Following pages: Shells with Ricotta and Fresh Vegetables

Tortellini with Cream, Ham and Peas

Excellent tortellini, filled with either meat or cheese, can be bought in most supermarkets and specialty food stores. This makes a very rich dish, perhaps best served as an appetizer before grilled fish or meat.

1 pound tortellini
1 tablespoon butter
1 cup fresh shelled peas
1/4 pound prosciutto or good baked ham, in julienne
1/2 cup light cream
1 teaspoon freshly ground black pepper

Cook the tortellini in gently boiling, salted water as per directions on the package.

Meanwhile, melt the butter in a small saucepan, add the peas, cover and cook over low heat for 10 minutes.

Uncover, add the ham and heat through, about 5 minutes. Finally, add the cream and heat to just the boiling point.

Pour over the hot tortellini, sprinkle with pepper and serve at once. Serves 4-6 as an appetizer.

Right: Tortellini with Cream, Ham and Peas

Preceding pages: Spaghetti Primavera

Pasta and Bean Soup

1 onion, finely chopped
1/4 pound bacon, cut into small dice
2 tablespoons olive oil
2 cloves garlic, chopped
4 cups chicken stock or canned broth
1 28-ounce can small cannellini beans
1 teaspoon hot pepper flakes
1/4 pound short tubular pasta

Sauté the onion and bacon in the olive oil, in a large saucepan adding the garlic after 3 minutes. Add the beans and pepper flakes and cook over low heat for 5 minutes stirring carefully (so as not to break the beans). Add the stock and simmer covered for 15 minutes. Finally, add the pasta and cook, uncovered until *al dente*, about 15 minutes more. Serves 4-6.

Preceding pages: Pasta and Bean Soup

Spinach Pasta with
Shrimp and Mushrooms

1/4 cup olive oil
3 cloves garlic, chopped
1/2 pound mushrooms, thinly sliced
1/2 pound shrimp, peeled, deveined and cut into quarters
1/4 cup dry white wine
1 tablespoon fresh basil, chopped
1 pound spinach pasta (linguine is good)

Sauté the garlic in the olive oil in a skillet until lightly
browned. Add the mushrooms and cook over high heat
just until the juices begin to emerge. Add the shrimp
and cook for 5 minutes. Now add the white wine and
basil and cook for 2 minutes more.

Meanwhile, cook the pasta until *al dente* and drain.
Pour the sauce over and serve. Serves 4.

Following pages: Spinach Pasta with Shrimp and Mushrooms

Rigatoni Siciliana

1/4 cup olive oil
2 cloves garlic, peeled and chopped
1 medium eggplant, peeled and
    cut into 1/2 inch cubes
1 28-ounce can plum tomatoes,
    drained and coarsely chopped
1/2 cup seedless white raisins
1/2 teaspoon red pepper flakes
1 pound rigatoni

In a large skillet, sauté the garlic in the olive oil over medium heat. Add the eggplant and continue cooking, stirring constantly, for 5 minutes until the eggplant is softened. Add the tomatoes and cook for 15 minutes.

Meanwhile, soak the raisins in hot water for 10 minutes. Drain.

Add the raisins and the red pepper flakes to the sauce and cook for five minutes more.

Cook the rigatoni in boiling, salted water until *al dente*. Drain. Pour the sauce over and serve. Serves 4.

Preceding pages: Rigatoni Siciliana

Spinach Fettucine with Mussels

4 pounds mussels, scrubbed and debearded
1 cup dry white wine
2 tablespoons olive oil
1 clove garlic, peeled and chopped
2 onion, peeled and sliced thinly
2 carrots, peeled and julienned
salt and pepper to taste
1 pound spinach fettucine

In a large pot, place the mussels and white wine. Steam, covered, stirring occasionally, until the shells open. When cool enough to handle, shell the mussels, reserving a dozen in their shells for garnishing. Strain the liquid from the mussels through cheesecloth and reserve.

In a large saucepan, sauté the garlic and onion in the olive oil until soft and golden. Add carrots and cook gently, until soft. Season with salt and pepper. Add the shelled mussels and just enough of the reserved liquid to moisten everything to a depth of about 1 inch. Heat through, but do not let boil or the mussels will toughen.

Meanwhile, cook the fettucine in boiling, salted water until done. Drain.

Pour the sauce over the pasta and toss well. Garnish with the reserved mussels in their shells. Serves 4.

Following pages: Spinach Fettucine with Mussels

Ravioli Siciliana

This rather bizarre-sounding dish is actually quite good and mingles the flavors of Italy with the Arab-influenced cuisine of Sicily.

2 tablespoons pine nuts
2 tablespoons olive oil
1 large onion, peeled and chopped
2 cloves garlic peeled and chopped
1 28-ounce can plum tomatoes, drained and chopped
1 large can skinless, boneless sardines, preferably in olive
    oil, drained and chopped
1/2 cup seedless white raisins, soaked for 10 minutes in
    hot water and drained
1 teaspoon red pepper flakes
1 pound small, cheese-stuffed ravioli

Place the pine nuts on a baking sheet and toast for 10 minutes in a medium oven. Remove, cool and set aside.

In a large skillet, sauté the onion and garlic in the olive oil over medium heat, until soft and golden. Add the tomatoes and simmer, stirring occasionally, for 10 minutes. Add the sardines, raisins and red pepper flakes and simmer for 10 minutes more.

Meanwhile cook the ravioli as per the instructions on the package. Drain. Top with the sauce and serve immediately. Serves 4.

Right: Ravioli Siciliana

Pasta with Spinach and Sausages

1 tablespoon butter
1 clove garlic, peeled and chopped
1/2 pound sweet or hot Italian sausage, removed from
    the casings
1 10-ounce package frozen chopped spinach, defrosted
1/2 cup light cream
1 pound rigatoni or penne

Sauté the garlic in the butter in a large skillet. When
lightly browned, add the sausage meat and cook over
medium heat, breaking up the sausage with a fork until
lightly browned and almost reduced to sausage
crumbs.

Add the spinach and mix well. Add the cream and
let heat through.

Meanwhile, cook the pasta in boiling, salted water.
Drain

Toss the pasta well with the sauce and serve at
once. Serves 4.

Preceding pages: Pasta with Spinach and Sausages

Orzo with Butter, Chopped Nuts and Mushrooms

Orzo is the tiny, grain-shaped pasta. It cooks very quickly and is perfect as a side-dish, to accompany roast or grilled meats.

4 tablespoons butter
1 clove garlic, peeled and chopped
1/2 pound mushrooms, roughly chopped
2 tablespoons walnuts or pecans, coarsely chopped
Pepper to taste
1 pound orzo

Melt the butter in a large skillet. Sauté the garlic and mushrooms until soft and lightly browned. Add the chopped nuts and heat through.

Meanwhile, cook the orzo in boiling, salted water. This should only take about 5 minutes. Drain.

Toss the orzo with the sauce. Serves 4.

Following pages: Orzo with Butter, Chopped Nuts and Musrooms

Rigatoni with Ragout

This is a dish to make when you are cooking a stew or pot roast (especially if flavored with red wine and herbs).

3 cups gravy from stew or pot roast
1 pound rigatoni
1/2 cup grated Parmesan cheese

Place the gravy in a small saucepan and cook over low heat, uncovered, for at least 1 hour, until the gravy is reduced to half its original volume.

Meanwhile, cook the rigatoni in boiling, salted water. Drain.

Toss the pasta with the gravy and 1/2 cup of grated Parmesan cheese. Serve more cheese on the side. Serves 4.

Preceding pages: Rigatoni with Ragout

Pasta Salad with Shrimp

1 pound medium shrimp, peeled and deveined
1 cup fresh raw peas
1 tablespoon chopped pimento
3/4 cup extra virgin olive oil
2 tablespoon wine vinegar
2 teaspoons Dijon mustard
1 pound penne or ziti, cooked and drained
salt and pepper to taste

Cook the shrimp in boiling, salted water for 3 minutes. Drain.

Toss the shrimp with the peas, pimento, olive oil, vinegar, mustard and salt and pepper to taste.

Add the pasta and toss well. Serve at room temperature. Serves 4-6.

Following pages: Pasta Salad with Shrimp

Farfalle with Peas and Bacon

1/4 pound pancetta or lightly smoked bacon, diced
1 clove garlic, peeled and chopped
1 cup fresh peas, shelled
3/4 cup chicken broth
1/2 cup grated Parmesan cheese
1 pound farfalle
pepper to taste

In a skillet fry the pancetta or bacon until the fat runs.
Add the garlic, peas and chicken broth and cook over a
low heat for 15 minutes, until the peas are tender and
the broth has reduced.

In the meantime, cook the farfalle in boiling, salted
water until *al dente*. Drain.

Pour the sauce over the pasta, add pepper to taste
and Parmesan cheese. Toss well. Serves 4.

Preceding pages: Farfalle with Peas and Bacon

Tortellini Salad

A delightful dish for lunch on a hot summer's day.

1 sweet red pepper, cored, seeded and julienned
1 green pepper, cored, seeded and julienned
1 small onion, peeled and finely chopped
2/3 cup olive oil
3 tablespoons wine vinegar
1/2 cup grated Parmesan cheese
salt and pepper to taste
1 pound cheese tortellini

Mix the red and green peppers, onion, olive oil, vinegar, cheese and salt and pepper to taste in a bowl.

Cook the tortellini in boiling, salted water until just tender. Drain

Toss the tortellini, hot, with the dressing and let stand at room temperature for 1 hour for the flavors to meld. Serves 4.

Following pages: Tortellini Salad

Orechiette with Sausage

Orechiette are "little ears" and are excellent with strong and spicy sauces.

1/4 cup olive oil
1/2 pound hot Italian sausage, skinned and broken up
1 clove garlic, peeled and chopped
1/4 cup dry white wine
1 large ripe tomato, peeled, seeded and roughly chopped
1 pound orechiette

In a large skillet heat the olive oil. Add the sausage and garlic and let sauté for about 10 minutes, until the sausage bits are cooked through. Add the white wine and let simmer for 5 minutes to reduce and thicken.

In the meantime cook the pasta in boiling, salted water until *al dente*. Drain.

Toss the pasta with the sauce. Sprinkle the raw tomato over the top. Serves 4.

Right: Orechiette with Sausage

Penne with Pesto

Pesto is the wonderful, *uncooked* sauce of Genoa and the Ligurian coast. There are dozens of recipes; all I can say is this one is authentic and good.

1 large bunch fresh basil
2-3 cloves garlic, peeled
1/4 cup pine nuts
1/4 cup Parmesan cheese or Parmesan and Romano mixed
2/3 cup extra virgin olive oil
1 pound penne
1/4 cup melted butter
pepper to taste

Place the basil (leaves only), garlic, pine nuts and cheese in the container of a food processor. Cover. Process, slowly adding the olive oil until a thick paste is achieved. Add pepper to taste.

In the meantime, cook the penne in boiling, salted water until *al dente*. Drain and toss with the melted butter. Place a spoonful of the pesto on each portion and serve with more cheese and butter. Each person mixes his or her own at the table. Serves 4.

Left: Penne with Pesto

Fresh Pasta

Pasta is not hard to make. You will need a large pastry board and a rolling pin and/or pasta rolling machine, like that pictured on the preceding pages.

The best flour is hard flour or what is increasingly sold as bread flour. Cake flour or other soft flours will not hold together and will make disintegrating, mushy pasta dough.

Here's a simple recipe for fettucine, the easiest of home made pastas.

4 level cups flour, sifted
2 large eggs
salt
water

Pour the flour onto the pastry board in a mound. Make a depression in the middle and break in the eggs. Add 1-2 teaspoons salt and 4-5 tablespoons cold water.

Now, fold the flour over the eggs, salt and water and knead the dough until it can be formed into a ball.

Continue to knead for about 10 minutes, folding the dough again and again until it is elastic. Remember to keep your hands and the board lightly floured.

Divide the dough ball in half. Roll out one piece with the rolling pin and continue to roll, flouring the board each time, until the dough is thinned out—8-10 rolls— and you can see the board underneath. Pick up the dough and lay over a cloth or chair back until it is dry, about 30 minutes. Repeat with the second half of the dough.

Now, roll up the sheets and cut into ribbons about 3/8-inch wide.

To cook, drop into a pan of boiling, salted water and cook for 2-3 minutes. Remember, nothing has to soften, so longer cooking will result in a mass of glutinous fragments. Serve with any sauce you choose or just with butter and cheese to really appreciate the taste of the fresh pasta. Serves 4-6.